Dinos

by Libby Romero

Table of Contents

Introduction

Tyrannosaurus rex was a **dinosaur**. Tyrannosaurus rex lived millions of years ago. Many other dinosaurs lived then.

What were dinosaurs? What happened to dinosaurs? How do we know about dinosaurs? Read this book to learn about dinosaurs.

Words to Know

 carnivores

 dinosaur

 extinct

 fossils

 herbivores

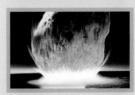 meteorite

 omnivores

 reptiles

See the Glossary on page 22.

What Were Dinosaurs Like?

Dinosaurs were **reptiles**. Dinosaurs had backbones. Dinosaurs had four legs.

Dinosaurs had scaly skin. They laid eggs.

▲ Dinosaurs laid eggs.

Try This

Use clay. Make a dinosaur model.
1. Make a backbone.
2. Make four legs.
3. Make scaly skin.

5

All dinosaurs lived on land.

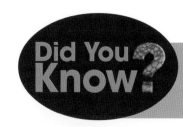

Flying reptiles were not dinosaurs.

▲ Dinosaurs lived on land.

Triceratops was a dinosaur. Triceratops had a backbone and four legs. Triceratops had four legs and laid eggs. Triceratops lived on land.

▲ Triceratops was a reptile.

It's A Fact

Dinosaurs lived on all the continents.

Some dinosaurs were **carnivores**. Carnivores ate meat. Carnivores ate other animals.

▲ Tyrannosaurus rex was a carnivore.

The largest dinosaurs were **herbivores**. Herbivores ate plants. Some dinosaurs were **omnivores**. Omnivores ate plants and meat.

▲ **Brachiosaurus was an herbivore.**

▲ **Oviraptor was an omnivore.**

What Happened to Dinosaurs?

Dinosaurs first lived 230 million years ago.

▲ Eoraptor was one of the first dinosaurs.

Then dinosaurs were **extinct**. All the dinosaurs died. Dinosaurs were extinct 65 million years ago.

Solve This

Dinosaurs first lived 230 million years ago. Dinosaurs were extinct 65 million years ago. How long did dinosaurs live on Earth?

Answer: 165 million years

▲ The dinosaurs died.

Why did the dinosaurs die? Scientists are not sure. Maybe dinosaurs could not find food.

▲ Maybe dinosaurs did not have food.

Maybe many volcanoes erupted. Dust and gases went into the air. The dust and gases blocked sunlight. Earth was colder.

▲ Maybe volcanoes erupted.

▲ Maybe Earth became colder. Plants and animals died.

14

Maybe a huge **meteorite** fell to Earth. Meteorite dust blocked the sunlight. Earth was colder. Plants and animals died.

▲ Maybe a meteorite fell to Earth.

How Do We Know About Dinosaurs?

People find **fossils** of dinosaurs. The fossils are from long ago. Fossils show us about dinosaurs.

▲ This man has a dinosaur bone fossil.

People find many types of fossils.

▲ People find dinosaur egg fossils.

▲ People find dinosaur footprints.

▲ People find many fossils.

People put dinosaur bone fossils together. The bones form dinosaur skeletons. We can see what dinosaurs were like.

▲ **People work with dinosaur bones.**

▲ **The bones form skeletons.**

Sue is a dinosaur skeleton. Sue is a Tyrannosaurus rex skeleton. Sue is the best Tyrannosaurus rex skeleton.

It's A Fact

A scientist named Sue Henderson found the dinosaur in South Dakota. People named the dinosaur Sue.

Learn More

Learn more about Sue.
Visit http://www.fieldmuseum.org/sue/.

19

Summary

Dinosaurs were reptiles. Dinosaurs first lived 230 million years ago. Dinosaurs were extinct 165 million years later. People find dinosaur fossils.

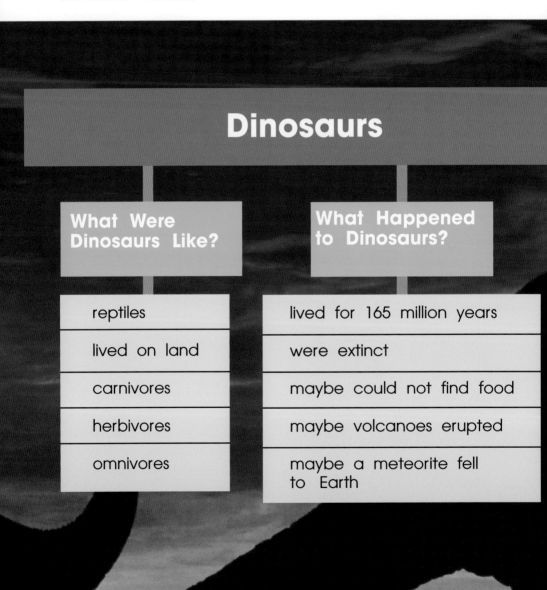

Dinosaurs

What Were Dinosaurs Like?	What Happened to Dinosaurs?
reptiles	lived for 165 million years
lived on land	were extinct
carnivores	maybe could not find food
herbivores	maybe volcanoes erupted
omnivores	maybe a meteorite fell to Earth

How Do We Know About Dinosaurs?

fossils

Think About It

1. What were dinosaurs like?
2. What happened to dinosaurs?
3. Fossils help us learn about dinosaurs. How?

21

Glossary

carnivores animals that eat meat

Many dinosaurs were ***carnivores***.

dinosaur a reptile that lived millions of years ago

The ***dinosaur*** *laid eggs.*

extinct all members of the species are dead

Dinosaurs are ***extinct***.

fossils remains of plants or animals from long ago

People find dinosaur ***fossils***.

herbivores animals that eat plants

*Some dinosaurs were **herbivores**.*

meteorite a piece of rock from outer space

*Maybe a **meteorite** fell to Earth.*

omnivores animals that eat meat and plants

*Some dinosaurs were **omnivores**.*

reptiles cold-blooded animals with a backbone and scaly skin

*Dinosaurs were **reptiles**.*

Index